A Guide to Acquiring an Astral Magic Wand

Immersive Magic, Volume 1

Merryl Kowalska

Published by Merryl Kowalska, 2022.

A GUIDE TO ACQUIRING AN ASTRAL MAGIC WAND

First edition. December 3, 2022.

ISBN: 979-8201147648

Written by Merryl Kowalska.

Also by Merryl Kowalska

Immersive Magic
A Guide to Acquiring an Astral Magic Wand

Table of Contents

Introduction.. 1

What is an Astral Magic Wand? 3

Two Types of Magic Wands.. 5

Finger Wand.. 7

How to Create Your Own Astral Wand........................ 9

Important Points to Know about Astral Wands 12

Meditation Practice 15

Basic Astral Wand.. 18

How to Take Care of Astral Magic Wands................... 22

The 4 Elemental Astral Wands.................................... 25

Basic Elemental Wand 30

How to Use an Astral Wand... 34

Random Astral Wand 37

The Solitary Wand 39

Wand of Terra 42

Ifrit Wand 45

Best Practices 48

A Call to Christ.. 51

For Lilith

Introduction

Immersive Magic: A Guide to Acquiring an Astral Magic Wand is a magical manual that teaches how you can acquire your very own astral magic wand. The magic wand is one of the most important tools of a magus. The astral magic wand is not an ordinary wand, but it is a magic wand that exists in the astral plane. The fact that it exists in the astral dimension makes it very practical for magical workers since it will allow you to use your wand anywhere, even in public.

Acquiring an astral wand is easy as long as you know how to do it properly. This magical practice will also develop your overall magical faculties.

Immersive Magic: A Guide to Acquiring an Astral Magic Wand discusses the steps that you need to know to own an astral wand. It also reveals the magical places that you can visit to claim certain wands, including rare types of magic wands. As an added bonus, we will also discuss how you can create your very own astral magic wand.

It should be noted that this book is not only about acquiring an astral wand, but you will also learn how to make use of your mind in a magical way, as well as how you can effectively journey into the magical realms that are beyond the physical dimension, among others. Indeed, this book presents a journey, but it is up to you to take the actual steps.

Immersive Magic: A Guide to Acquiring an Astral Magic Wand is written in a simple, direct, and easy-to-follow format, so that you can easily focus on learning and experiencing the magic that has been long hidden away from prying eyes.

Are you ready to claim your very own astral wand? Are you ready to learn real magic? If yes, then welcome into this magical universe, for your magical journey shall now begin.

What is an Astral Magic Wand?

There are two keywords to understanding an astral magic wand: *magic wand* and *astral*. A magic wand is a basic tool of a magical practitioner. It is usually in the form of a short stick, but even a long stick is sometimes also used. A magic wand can help direct magical energy, and it is often used in magical rituals and workings that involve direct energy manipulation.

A magic wand, or simply called *wand*, can also possess certain energy qualities and powers. For example, a fire magic wand can more effectively harness the element of fire than other elemental wands, and a healing wand can summon powerful healing energies. As you can see, having a wand can be very helpful for a magical worker.

A magic wand usually has a physical form. However, there are also the so-called *astral wands*, and they are the kind of magic wand that is the subject of this book. An astral wand is a magic wand that exists only in the astral plane. Although it exists only in the astral plane, it is also as effective (or even more effective) than a physical magic wand.

But what is the astral plane? The astral plane is another dimension of existence. While the physical world is composed of physical things and bodies, the astral plane is the realm of thoughts, ideas, spirits, and the imagination. It co-exists with the physical world. Just as the physical body belongs to the physical plane, the soul resides in the astral plane. It should be clarified that the physical world and the astral plane are not completely separate from each other. In fact, they affect and influence each other. For example, various occult studies and experiments have shown that before a disease has any manifestation in the physical world, it first manifests and has its existence in the astral plane. Making changes in the astral plane also creates changes in the physical plane, and vice versa.

So why would you like to have an astral magic wand? An astral magic wand can give you power. It also helps in the manipulation of magical energy. A wand can magnify your current energy power and make your magic significantly more effective and powerful.

It is worth noting that an astral magic wand can be as effective as a physical magic wand. In fact, depending on the wand that you have, an astral wand can even be more effective and powerful than a physical wand. Having an astral wand will also allow you to bring it with you anywhere, as well as use it and work your magic even in public without getting noticed by anyone.

Two Types of Magic Wands

There are two types of magic wands: the living wands and the non-living wands. The living wands are naturally imbued with life while the non-living wands do not have life and are charged only with magical energy. Take note that this does not mean that a living wand is always stronger than a non-living wand. It still depends on the particular wand that you have. This categorization of a living and non-living wand applies to both physical wands and astral magic wands.

Living wands come directly from a source that has life. Moreover, living wands have a living spirit or at least a living element within it. Therefore, it is clear that a living wand has life, for it is also inhabited with life.

Non-living wands do not come from a source of life and are not inhabited by any spirit, being, or element. These kinds of magic wands usually come from an intentional creation of a magus. Simply put, it can be said that living wands are natural while non-living wands are artificial.

Non-living wands are usually created in the physical plane. However, it should be noted that there are also living wands that may originate directly from the physical plane. As you can see, to date, we have a vast world to explore when it comes to magic wands, which makes this journey even more exciting.

Based on the aforesaid differences, it may appear that a living wand is much better than a non-living wand. However, this is not always the case. Throughout history, there have been non-living wands that are simply remarkable. These wands are usually those that were made by very advanced practitioners of magic or by very fine and master craftsmen of magic wands. This only goes to show that although living wands are generally preferable over non-living wands, such may not always be the case since there can be certain exceptions.

Finger Wand

To give you an idea of how a magic wand works, here is a simple exercise that you can try. For this exercise, you are going to use the most basic and natural wand that you already have — your finger. It is preferable to use the index finger, but any finger will do. The steps are as follows:

Extend your finger and gently focus on it. Now, blow on your finger. Know that breath is energy, and that breath is life. As you blow into your finger, see and feel that your finger is absorbing all the magical energy of breath into itself. Do this for about 10 breaths/blows.

Next, position your hands so that your finger wand is pointing at the palm of your other hand. There is no strict position on how this is to be done, but the point here is simply to point your finger wand at the palm of your other hand since you are going to send energy to it.

You are now going to send the accumulated energy in your finger wand to your other hand. Imagine a ray of white light pouring from your finger wand onto the center of the palm of your other hand. See and feel the energy projecting from your finger wand and going toward your other hand. Keep sending energy to the same point at the center of your palm and accumulate all the energy there.

Do you feel the projected energy with your other hand? Do not try or force yourself to feel something. Instead, just relax and keep an open mind as you project energy to your hand. If done correctly, you should be able to feel the projected energy with your other hand. To end this simple exercise, simply shake your hands to disperse whatever energy that may have accumulated in them.

The aforementioned exercise is a good way to be familiar with energy, as well as a good brief introduction to the magic wand. With the use of a finger wand, you are able to concentrate the energy that you are projecting. It is also easier to harness energy with a wand, even with just a basic finger wand.

If a simple finger wand can be this helpful, just imagine the wonders that will be possible for you once you get your hands on other more useful magic wands, especially the living astral wands. Indeed, the powers that you can harness and the possibilities that will open themselves before you shall be limitless and infinite.

How to Create Your Own Astral Wand

Let us now talk about creating your very own astral wand. If it is your first time to have a magic wand, then you might find this technique really interesting. It is also a simple and effective technique that you can do even if you are just a beginner in the magical arts.

We have to understand that the mind can be harnessed in a magical way — and once harnessed in this manner, you can create real changes, and even put into existence a new magic wand.

You are now going to create your own astral wand. As an astral wand, it is a wand that exists in the astral plane. This wand is a non-living wand. Nevertheless, it can still be a powerful wand, depending on how well you create it, as well as how you wield it. Having said that, the steps are as follows:

Imagine what your astral wand would look like. If you are the artistic type, you might want to draw it on paper. Next, just close your eyes and imagine your astral wand. See it right in front of you amid the pitch darkness. Know that every imaginary creation has its existence in the astral realm. Now, move your hand and pick up the astral wand. To be able to do this, use your imagination. Now, see and feel that you are now holding your wand with your hand.

The next step is to name your astral wand. Naming a wand is not always necessary, but it still helps especially if you keep several wands. It also helps to further impress the existence of your astral wand. After all, almost everything in this world that exists has a name, or at least we tend to call something by a name. Names also have power. This is a well-established teaching in the magical arts. Simply by calling your wand by its name, you can summon it instantly.

Naming a wand is very easy and straightforward. Simply tell it its name. For example, "I name you ____________." You can also say, "Your name is ____________." Say this thrice to impress the name upon your wand. When choosing a name, the recommended practice is to use a name that other people will not be able to guess easily. Again, names have power. You do not want other witches or wizards to take control of your wand by summoning it by its name.

After naming your wand, the next step is to charge your astral wand with energy. There are many ways to do this. If you have basic knowledge on energy manipulation, you are free to apply whatever energy-charging technique that you know. If you are a complete beginner, then you can use the following method:

Imagine your wand in front of you. Position your hands in a blessing position, palms facing the wand. Now, Imagine magical energy around you. You are free to imagine magical energy in any form you want. It is recommended to visualize magical energy as white light all around you. Next, using your imagination, see and feel that you are drawing the universal white light energy toward your astral wand, and then pour that energy into your wand. Continue to pour energy into your wand, thereby making it stronger and stronger. Once you are satisfied with the power hat you have imbued into your wand, hold it in your hand, and use it as you would any other magic wand. You can use it to help direct magical energy. You can also use the energy that is charged within the wand for any magical work. For now, just focus on learning to create an astral magic wand. The aforementioned practice will also develop your skills in the fine magical art of energy manipulation.

Important Points to Know about Astral Wands

As a magical practitioner, you should have the right foundational knowledge about astral wands. Although they are similar to physical wands, they have some very interesting and even unusual qualities that you should know.

An astral wand can either be a living magic wand or a non-living wand. Many astral wands are living wands, except those that have been deliberately created. Now, there is this aspect that you should take note of: Unlike a physical want, an astral magic wand can have different users all at the same time. This may seem surprising, but it is actually in accordance with the laws of the magical realms, which makes it possible. This means that the same wand can be used by more than two people at the same time. There are only very few exceptions to this, such as in the case of some rare astral wands that are exclusively limited to a single user each time.

Just like other astral creations, astral magic wands also require magical energy. If you do not know it yet, it is actually a basic principle in magic that all things, visible and invisible, are made of magical energy. It is also important to charge your astral wand with energy to keep it in the best condition to do whatever task you give to it.

Newly-made wands are prone to disappearing or disintegrating. As a rule, a wand has to be recharged with energy daily; otherwise, it will disappear into nothingness (by joining the energy matrix). Therefore, if you want to keep your newly-made wand for a long period, be sure to recharge it with energy at least once daily. If it runs out of energy, it will simply fade on its own. However, wands that have lasted for 40 days are believed to gain the ability of being permanent. They will no longer fade into nothingness but retain its existence as a wand. Therefore, if you want to keep a wand for a long period, be sure to recharge it at least once daily with energy for 40 consecutive days. Back in the 12th century, it was believed that 20 days would be enough, but this theory was soon modified into 40 days sometime in the 16 century. Personally, I concur with the view of 40 days since it is also in accordance with other universal laws, as well as the significance of the number 40 in various occult sciences and even in the Christian scriptures.

Interestingly, many wands that you can get from the astral world are living wands and have long been in existence already. So, most of these wands would not require any 40-day maintenance. Still, if you want any wand to be in top condition for magical work, you must recharge your wand with energy regardless whether it has reached the 40-day maintenance period or not.

Recharging a wand with energy is simple. It follows the very same technique as when you charge a wand that you have created for the first time where you simply pour magical energy into it. And, since magical energy is abundant all around you, you would not have any problem with this. It is just really up to you to take good care of your magic wand.

There are countless astral magic wands in the universe, and there are many more that are being born and created. There are also some rare types of astral wands, and we will discuss some of them later in this book, as well as how you can obtain them.

In the world of magic wands, both for physical and astral wands, there is a belief that there is one particular wand that is meant for every wizard/witch. Although it is not uncommon for magical practitioners to have several wands in their possession, there is one special wand for each of us — and it is this wand that will teach the magus to unleash his ultimate power. However, finding this single wand is where the challenge is. It is said that in the end, it is actually the wand that finds you once you are ready.

Meditation Practice

Before you engage in the actual steps in acquiring an astral wand, it is good to first acquire the right state of mind. It should be noted that, as a basic working principle in magical arts, all true and genuine magic starts and ends in the mind. Therefore, it is important you develop the right mindset for magical work. This applies whether you are engaged in acquiring a wand or not, as long as you are engaged in any magical work. The reason for this is that all magic is of the mind; hence, the occult saying, "The All is Mind; the Universe is Mental."

When it comes to acquiring the magical mindset, which is the mindset that is optimum for magical work, the practice of meditation is very important. In fact, it is a basic rule in magic that one who truly wants to attain real and significant progress must meditate at least twice daily. Meditation is a natural and effective technique to develop your overall spiritual and psychic faculties.

Contrary to what many people think, the practice of meditation is actually very easy and simple. In fact, it is more about not doing anything rather than having to do something. After all, meditation involves stilling and calming the mind. Your mind is already very powerful as it is right now; you just have to break down the walls that you have built which limit its power.

So how do you meditate? There are countless ways to meditate, but you do not really need to learn them. This is because all meditation techniques lead to one and the same path, and that is the path of spiritual enlightenment and magical development. You do not even need to have to force it, for meditation itself will naturally make this happen.

The meditation technique that you are about to learn is a basic mantra meditation. A mantra is a word, syllable, phrase, set of words, or a sound that functions as the point of focus in meditation. It helps to quiet the mind. Instead of the mind being scattered to so many thoughts and ideas, you will be able to concentrate it into a single thought—and in this case, it is the mantra.

The mantra that you are going to use is the mantra *Maranatha*. This mantra is not an ordinary mantra, for it is already charged with so much spiritual and divine energy because it has been used by various practitioners for centuries. The word *Maranatha* is actually a word in the Aramaic language, which is the language that is believed to have been spoken by the Divine Master, Jesus Christ, when He walked the earth. In English, it means, *Come, Lord, come, Lord Jesus.*

You do not really need to be a true believer in Jesus Christ before you can use and benefit from this mantra. The word itself has already become a power word, a source of divine power. Once you use it, regardless of your beliefs, you can enjoy the benefits that it offers. Having said that, here are the steps:

Make sure that you will not be disturbed for some time. It is good to meditate in a solitary place. You do not really need to go outside as you can also meditate in your room or anywhere where you will not be disturbed by anything and anyone.

A GUIDE TO ACQUIRING AN ASTRAL MAGIC WAND

Assume a comfortable position and relax. Close your eyes and do not think about anything. Just allow your mind to be free. This is not the time to think and worry. If thoughts arise in the mind, which they usually do, simply ignore them gently. You must not employ any kind of force during meditation. If you are tempted to think, know that the time to think is not during meditation, but after the meditation.

Now, slowly recite your mantra: *Maranatha*. Say it gently and lovingly. You may say your mantra like a whisper or even in your mind only. As you say your mantra, gently focus on it in exclusion of all other thoughts and things. Only the mantra must exist in your mind. Be one with your mantra. Become the mantra.

Continue the meditation for as long as you like. At any time that you want to end the meditation, simply bring your awareness back to your physical body, slowly move your fingers and toes, and then very gently open your eyes with a smile.

The practice of meditation can be said to be a necessity if you truly want to attain a higher state of mind and being. It is also recommended to meditate before you engage in any magical work because meditation prepares the mind for the tasks that you are about to do. From now on, make the practice of meditation a priority in your life. The more that you meditate, the more that you will improve and reach a higher state of mind. Always remember that practice makes perfect.

Basic Astral Wand

Now that you have a good foundational knowledge, it is time to get into the actual practice of acquiring your first astral wand that is from the universe (not created by you). It should be noted that there are many astral wands in the universe. In fact, there are more astral wands than physical wands. For your very first astral wand from the universe, it is good to start with the basic astral wand, which is also the easiest to obtain.

In this exercise, you are going to access the magical realm, and you will get your wand there. Do not worry, this is easy to do. The steps are very simple, but just make sure to practice regularly. There are three key points that you need for this magic to work. First, you must be able to access the magical realm. Second, you must go to a place in the magical realm that has an astral magic wand. And lastly, you must be able to acquire the wand. Having said that, here are the steps:

Assume a comfortable position and relax. Close your eyes and clear your mind. Although not necessary, you might want to start with a few minutes of meditation to ease the mind into the right mindset. Next, with your eyes closed and mind open, imagine a beautiful forest right in front of you. Know in your mind that this is the Forest of Wands. It is a magical forest in the astral realm that is dedicated to magic wands. All the trees in this forest drop magic wands from time to time. You may even see some wands just lying on the ground. You are free to take one every visit.

A GUIDE TO ACQUIRING AN ASTRAL MAGIC WAND

Before stepping into the forest, talk to the forest first and tell the forest your intention, and be sure to tell the forest that you come in peace and mean no harm.

Take note that this forest has eyes everywhere. Be sure to follow the rules and only take one magic wand per visit. If you are wondering what the consequence might be for violating this simple rule, then legend has it that he who violates the rule shall lose his life equivalent to 500 days. Hence, every violation will be meted with a 500-day penalty, charged on your total lifespan on Earth. So, in case of violation, you will be losing about more than a year of life, but less than two years. However, this is only for one violation. The penalty will keep adding up for every violation.

Imagine walking into the forest. Now, pay attention to your surroundings. What do you see? Look at the trees around you and the ground. You might find a magic wand lying somewhere. This is the Forest of the Wands, a forest that is full of magic wands of various kinds. Back in the Old Days, legend has it that two very rare wands were found in this forest. If you are lucky, you might still be able to find a rare wand here.

Instead of hurrying to get a wand, it is recommended to first get used to the place. Just walk around the forest and appreciate the beautiful scenery. If you see other magical beings, just ignore them for now.

Once you are more familiar with the forest, go ahead and focus on finding a magic wand for yourself. It is not uncommon to find many wands here just lying on the ground under the trees.

To easily find a wand, just go where the trees are because the wands in this place come from the trees. Therefore, where there are more trees, there will also be more magic wands.

Once you find a wand to your liking, feel free to take it with you. If the wand is found under a tree or from a tree itself, be sure to ask permission from the tree before you get the wand. In the astral sphere, you can easily communicate through telepathy or simply by talking out loud as we normally do. However, in receiving messages, especially from trees, their usual mode of communication is through telepathy; therefore, it is important to keep an open mind at all times so that you could perceive whatever messages the trees might communicate to you.

Once you have your wand, you can now return to your physical body. Returning to your body is easy. Simply think of your physical body and use your willpower to return. Once you can sense your physical body, gently move your fingers and toes, and very gently open your eyes.

As soon as you open your eyes, look at the astral magic wand that you are holding in your hand. Since you are now back in the physical dimension, you will have to use your imagination to get a hold of the astral wand. Imagine that you are holding it with your hand. See and feel it in your hand.

Congratulations - you now have a real astral magic wand that is fresh from the universe.

A GUIDE TO ACQUIRING AN ASTRAL MAGIC WAND

The next important step is to name your new astral magic wand. As we have already discussed, this is as simple as telling it its name, such as, "I name you ___________," or "Your name is ___________." Repeat this at least thrice, and be sure not to forget the name of your new astral magic wand.

Feel free to visit the Forest of Wands at any time you want and as many times as you like. If you are a beginner, it is suggested that you take a trip to the Forest of Wands at least once daily. You do not need to bring a wand with you every time. Just enjoy the magical adventure. This practice will also develop your magical skills, which would be necessary for the other magical workings that you will be doing, especially once you set out in the search for a rare magic wand.

How to Take Care of Astral Magic Wands

If you engage in the magic art of magic wands, you must know how to take good care of your wands. Taking care of astral wands is easy as long as you know the right steps and measures to take.

After acquiring an astral magic wand, the first recommended step is to cleanse it. This is true even if you acquire a physical wand. Now, you may skip this part if you feel that the wand is cleansed already. After all, cleansing is just a magical method of removing negative energies. Therefore, if the wand is already free from negativity, then you may skip the cleansing stage. However, for physical magic wands, cleansing is strongly recommended all the time for all newly-acquired wands.

So, how do you cleanse an astral magic wand? Cleansing an astral wand is easy, and there are so many ways to do it. The technique that you are about to learn is one of the simplest and most effective ways to do it, and it is also the technique that is used by many astral magic wand owners, as well as advanced magical practitioners. Here are the steps:

Hold your wand in your hand. Now, see and feel a powerful ray of light falling from heaven. See and feel this ray of light pouring and bathing your magic wand with its powerful energy. As you are doing this, imagine all negativity from your wand being cleansed and completely removed. You should be able to see your wand lighting up with fresh white brilliance. This will happen automatically and naturally in your imagination as you cleanse your astral wand.

Keep bathing your wand with this powerful healing energy from heaven. Know that it is made of pure and powerful healing energy. Everything it touches heals. It is a powerful divine power.

Once you feel that your wand has been completely cleansed and charged with healing energy, you can now use your wand for whatever purpose you desire, and know that it is now free from all negative influences.

The next thing that you need to master is recharging your astral wand. Again, this is very easy. Simply hold your astral magic wand in your hand, and then imagine universal energy all around you. See and feel that you are drawing this universal energy toward you, and then pour it into your astral wand. Keep charging your wand with enough energy to fully recharge it. For new astral wands, it is good to always observe the 40-day rule on charging a wand to make the existence of the astral wand permanent in the astral dimension.

Another thing that you need to know is how to keep your astral magic wand. When it comes to keeping or storing your astral wand, there is a big difference between a physical wand and an astral wand. Keeping an astral wand is so much easier because you do not really need to keep it in any specific space. In fact, you can just let it go, and then you can call upon it at any time.

You might be wondering where astral wands go if you just drop them or make them vanish after using them. There are two schools of thought on this subject. One school of thought says that it goes back where you first found them. And, in the case of intentionally-created wands, they go back to the place where you first created them. The other school of thought believes that the astral wands remain with the magus/witch. The wands may become part of his natural energy or be hidden somewhere within his sphere of energy field. There is actually another school of thought, and it posits that the wand actually remains anywhere in the universe like a mere floating energy that is freely in the air or space. It just floats without any specific direction to take until the magus calls it back again.

Regardless which school of thought you would like to believe in, the important point here is that you can easily call on your wand at any time. This can be done easily by calling it by its name or simply by thinking about it and willing it to appear in your hand.

If you have a living wand, remember that it is very much alive. Living wands are also inhabited by a spirit, entity, or any other being that has life. It is recommended that you form a bond with whatever might be inhabiting your living wand. There are no hard and fast rules on this matter, but a good rule of thumb is to always use your living wand and to talk or connect with the spirit/entity that lives in the wand. This will help form a stronger bond with your magic wand, which will make it significantly more effective and powerful.

The 4 Elemental Astral Wands

The four elemental astral wands are astral magic wands that belong to their respective element in the universe. The four elemental powers are: fire, water, air, and earth. These are also the elements of the universe. Each element has its own unique magical qualities and properties, and we are going to discuss them one by one. Even if you are not into magic wands, it is important that you are familiar with the four elements. According to the ancient alchemists, everything in the universe is composed of at least one of the four elements. Human beings are one of the rarest kinds for we are made of all the four elements combined while many other things and beings in creation have less than four elements only.

It should be noted that the four elements are very much alive. They are living forces in this universe. The elements are also not limited to their physical manifestation. Therefore, the element of fire is not just the physical plane as we know it, but it also encompasses many qualities and properties, such as courage and sex, among others. By learning about the powers of the elements, one can wield an even greater power. And, if you master the art of wielding an elemental astral wand, the doors of magic shall open right before you. Having said that, let us discuss the elements and their magical qualities and properties.

Fire

The element of fire is said to be the first element in creation. Hence, it is written, *God said, "Let there be light."* Light rightly belongs to the fire element. Without the fire element, light could not exist. Here are the essential qualities and properties of the fire element:

- South direction
- Heat
- Sex
- Romance
- Strong will and determination
- Light
- Eyes
- Salamanders
- Passion
- War
- Anger
- Electric
- Red
- Courage

Water

According to the ancient alchemists, fire could not exist just on its own without the existence of the water element, just as water could not exist without fire. The water element is known for its powerful healing energy. Let us have a closer look at its wondrous powers and qualities:

- Healing

- Cleansing

- Beauty

- Blue

- Emotion

- Undines

- West direction

- Flexibility

- Stomach

- Magnetic

Air

The element of air is another interesting element. We are able to breathe because of this element. Although our eyes do not usually see it, it is nevertheless real and very important for survival. It also teaches us that there are important things in life that could not be seen by the eyes. Here are the fascinating attributes and qualities of the air element:

- Breathing

- East direction

- Movement

- Travel

- White

- Communication

- Sylphs

- Invisibility

- Levitation

Earth

The earth element is the element that is dear and very close to us, humans, for we are of the Earth. We are a natural part of the Earth. Since we have been born into this world, we have been swimming in the rich green energy of Mother Earth. Here are the wondrous qualities and properties of the earth element:

- North direction

- Manifestation

- Gnomes

- Strong foundation

- Natural instinct

- Survival

A GUIDE TO ACQUIRING AN ASTRAL MAGIC WAND

- Green

- Materialization

Having a good understanding of the elements will allow you to know which element you should use to create the change that you want to manifest. By using a wand that belongs to the element that is right for your current situation, you can harness real power more effectively.

Basic Elemental Wand

Are you ready to acquire your first real elemental astral wand. An astral elemental wand is an astral wand that is charged with a particular element. For example, a fire wand is charged with the element of fire, and a water wand is charged with the element of water. Basic elemental wands are easy to acquire if you know the right way to do it.

Acquiring an elemental astral wand includes journeying into the world of the particular element that you want to work with. For example, if you want to acquire an earth wand, then you will have to go into the world of the earth element. This way, the wands that you will find will often be a wand that is charged with the earth element.

Simply put, the key here is to go into the world of the element of your choice, and then acquire your wand from there. But how do you visit the world of the elements? The key lies in the power of your imagination. You have to understand that in the magical universe, the imagination plays a very important role. In fact, it can be said that without the imagination, there could also be no magic. Indeed, magic and imagination go hand in hand. But why is this so? Here is the occult secret: imagination is real.

The best way to learn to acquire an elemental wand is through actual practice. Having said that, here are the steps:

Assume a comfortable position and relax. Close your eyes and free the mind. Do not think about anything. You might want to meditate for a few minutes to help prepare your mind for the magical work that you are about to do. Just relax and let go.

Let us say that you are going to acquire a water astral wand. Imagine yourself in the water element. There are no hard and fast rules on how to do this, but a good way is to imagine yourself in the very center of a deep ocean. Know that you are in the universe of the water element. See and feel yourself in the deep ocean. You are a friend to this element. And, since you are not in your physical body, you are not limited by physical limitations. See and feel yourself underwater, and you can quickly move and breathe easily.

Before you move ahead on your journey, make your presence known to the water element first. It already knows that you are there, but it still helps to show respect by communicating your greeting and telling your intention. You can do this out loud or in your mind only.

After the initial introduction, just enjoy the universe of the water element. Look around you and explore the place. What do you see? Do you see fish and other water creatures and spirits? If you are lucky, you might also see a mermaid and other mythical creatures. Yes, these beings are very real, especially in the astral dimension where they usually thrive.

Once you are familiar with the place and feel more comfortable, you can now focus more on looking for an astral magic wand. Since you are in the very territory of the water element, you can be sure that the wands that you will find will very often belong to the water element.

You may find a wand on the ground, moving aimlessly in the water, or perhaps in a shell. Do not try to control anything. Just keep your mind open as you look around you.

If you are lucky enough and find a wand, feel free to take it. The recommended practice is to take only one wand for every visit. Once you obtain your wand, you can continue to spend more time in the universe of the water element or just return to your body.

To return to your body at any time, simply think of your body and use your willpower to bring yourself back. Once you can sense your body, slowly move your fingers and toes, and then very gently open your eyes, and look at the astral water magic wand that you are now holding in your hand.

The next step is to name your new elemental astral wand. You already know how to do this by now, and you know just how easy it is. It is as simple as telling your wand its name. It is also a good practice to observe the 40-day charging rule if you intend to keep your wand for a long time. Many elementary astral wands already have the ability of permanence, but it is still good to follow the 40-day rule just to be sure.

The same principle and similar technique applies if you want to work on another elemental wand. However, instead of imagining a body of water, see and feel yourself exposed to the environment of the element that you want to work with. For example, if you want to work with the element of fire, then imagine yourself in the center of the Sun. If you want to obtain an air wand, imagine yourself in the sky with the strong winds. If you want to acquire an earth astral wand, then imagine yourself in a rich forest.

33

How to Use an Astral Wand

You can use an astral wand in the same way that you use a physical wand. A wand will naturally help you in directing and controlling energy. For example, if you want to send energy to a particular point or location, you can simply point your wand in that direction, and you could already feel that you are more easily able to send energy to the said direction or specific point that you want. All wands can assist you in doing this.

Let us now talk about a more useful application of a magic wand, and that is using the power that a wand possesses. This is where magic wands differ from one another.

The first thing that you want to know is the quality of the energy that the wand is charged with. For example, if the wand is charged with the energy of healing, then you know that it can be used for healing magic. If the wand is charged with the power of the fire element, then you know that it can be used whenever you may need the qualities and properties of the fire element.

Once you know the power that your wand is charged with, then it is time to harness its power. This is actually easy to do since wands are magical tools that are almost alway self-working. The only challenging part is acquiring a wand; but once you have it, using it is a breeze. Simply hold the wand in your hand, and then imagine harnessing directly harnessing the energy of the wand itself. The wand becomes an extension of your hand, of your own psyche, and it possesses a specific energy quality or power that you can harness at any time.

f you are sensitive enough, you may notice that the energy that
s being projected from the wand has significantly more power
han the usual energy that you can harness from the universe.
This is one of the benefits of using a magic wand: its energy is
simply much more concentrated; and therefore, more powerful.
This is true, especially when you make the energy pass through
the tip of the wand, where energy can be highly focused and
concentrated.

Simply put, you can harness the energy of the wand directly by
making its energy flow from the wand and out through the tip
of the wand to the intended area or point. You can also wave the
wave and use that as the gesture of sending the wand's energy to
whatever point or direction that you want. You can easily assist
or guide how you want the energy to move or what you would
want it to do for you with your magical imagination. See and feel
the wand's energy, and imagine how it is moving to do your will.
At the magical moment, the wand becomes an extension of the
hand. It can be said that the wand becomes one of your fingers or
that the wand becomes your hand. Feel free to use it and do with
it as you will.

As you can see, a wand has many uses. There are really no hard
and fast rules. You can use your mind in creative ways as well.
It is also worth noting that a true wand, whether physical or
astral, can hold an enormous amount of energy. Do not think
that because of a wand's limited size that it cannot contain so
much energy. In fact, a well-charged wand can contain energy
that can be used for usual magical works for a month without
being recharged. There are even wands that hold so much energy
that you do not need to recharge them even for years. The reason

for this is that the energy in magic wands usually has a very high quality, and it is very concentrated.

The energy of a wand is also not limited by the size of a wand. In fact, the size of a wand has no relation to the energy that it holds. This is even truer when you are using an astral wand. Even a wand that is only an inch long can have the power that is needed to move the whole Earth and even the stars.

There are really no hard and fast rules on how to use a wand. Feel free to use your imagination and exercise your creativity without limitations. It is your wand, after all, so use it however and in whatever way you want.

Random Astral Wand

You can easily acquire a random astral wand by going to the astral dimension. If you look around, you may find some wands just lying around. Although you will likely encounter common wands most of the time, it is still possible to come across some rare living wands if you get lucky enough.

Random astral wands are the most common wands that magical practitioners depend on. It is just a matter of luck. You go to the astral sphere and see whatever wand may appear to you. It is also a fun and exciting experience.

Going to the astral dimension is easy. It is just a matter of using your imagination. Just be open to the magic of the universe. The flow of eternal magic is continuous and wonderful. The key is to align yourself to the beautiful rhythm of nature, and let go.

Make it a regular practice to visit the astral realm every now and then. You can easily do this by imagining a magical place or a beautiful forest. Another way to do this is simply to be open, and just go wherever your imagination leads you. The imagination is the key to access the astral dimension. The more that you use it, the more effective that you will be able to travel into the various levels of existence in the astral sphere.

You are free to collect as many astral wands as you like; but just be sure to take note of the wands in your collection. A good practice is by writing their names and descriptions in a notebook or journal. If you know how to draw, you can also draw your wands. Drawing your wands is also a good way to further impress their existence.

There are many interesting astral magic wands out there. So, the next time you visit the astral sphere, be sure to watch for astral wands along the way.

The Solitary Wand

The Solitary Wand is considered a rare wand. It can be found in the magical Desert of Eponin. It is a place in the astral dimension known for spiritual illumination and divine enlightenment. If you are the type who likes to wonder and reflect on various things, then you might want to get your hands on the Solitary Wand.

It is a rare wand because you will be able to find various wands in the Desert of Eponin, but it can be quite difficult to spot a real solitary wand. You will know that you have encountered a solitary wand because unlike the other wands in the said desert, the solitary wand glows in the night, and it releases a powerful energy that will definitely bring you peace and serenity. If you are being bombarded by so many negative thoughts and stresses, then you will definitely find the solitary wand really helpful. Having said that, let us now discuss the steps:

Assume a comfortable position and relax. Close your eyes and free the mind. Do not think about anything. You are now going to adventure into the so-called Desert of Eponin. It is a desert of magic and solitude. The way to travel into this wonderful desert is with the mind, and it is through the magical use of the imagination.

The Desert of Eponin has many faces. It is believed that the desert reveals itself to the magus once the magus is ready for it. The desert has a special fondness to those who are into magic wands simply because the Desert of Eponin is precisely about magic wands. If you have love for magic wands, then rest assured that you are welcome into this magical desert.

Take a few moments to just relax. Once the mind is clear, say the name of this magical desert together with your desire to see it, such as by saying, "Desert of Eponin, please reveal yourself to me." It is worth noting that the Desert of Eponin is very much alive, and it answers to the calls of a magus. Just keep your mind open. Now, gently chant the name of the desert, "Desert of Eponin, Desert of Eponin..."

Do you see an image of a desert in your mind's eye? If no, just keep chanting and desiring to be in this magical desert. Once it reveals itself to you, relax and just explore it.

Know that this desert is very much alive, and it holds great and wonderful magic. If you see magical beings around like faeries and the pixies, feel free to greet them. You can also talk to the desert. It should be noted that beings in the magical dimension often communicate via telepathy, so you should keep your mind open and watch out for any messages or communications that may be sent to you.

Once you are more familiar with the place, you can now go and search for your Solitary Wand. This Solitary Wand lies in the east side of the desert. Just head east. You will soon find yourself on a shore. If you look around you, you will find a small house. Go into this house, and you will find a chest in the corner. The Solitary Wand lies in this chest. It has a black color with a small dark crystal on one end. Once you see it, just take it with you. After all, it is an astral living wand. It can be used by various magicians and witches even at the same time. But only he who knows the way into the Desert of Eponin and into this little house can find it.

As soon as you get your Solitary Wand, you can now bring it with you as you return to your body. As soon as you return to the physical plane, be sure to give your Solitary Wand a name as this will distinguish it from the other magical practitioners who are also using it.

The Solitary Wand is known for its very peaceful and tranquil energy. Its energy will give you peace of mind and help you think more clearly. It also possesses healing energy. If you ever find this wand, then congratulations on acquiring one of the rare wands in the universe. Enjoy!

Wand of Terra

The Wand of Terra is the wand of the Earth. It is a wand that i̶ filled with the earth element. As such, it has all the earth elemen̶ qualities that you may need, such as stability, strong foundation̶ survival, healing, grounding, and materialization, among many̶ others.

This wand can be found in Middle Earth. To access the location̶ of this wand, you must first pass through the Dungeon of̶ Dismay. Do not worry, this is not difficult to do as long as you know the right steps to take. Having said that, here are the instructions to acquire the Wand of Terra, which is another rare astral magic wand:

Assume a comfortable position and relax. Close your eyes and free the mind. Once you are feeling relaxed, imagine a portal of blue light right in front of you. Next, enter this portal of light and immerse yourself into it. See and feel that you have been transported in a deserted field; and right in front of you lies a dark dungeon. This is the Dungeon of Dismay. Many untrained magicians and seekers have entered this Dungeon without ever returning. The key lies in a simple magical chant: *Emeno Extrosa*. Remember this as this will save your soul, as well as lead you toward the Wand of Terra, which is one of the greatest earth wands in the universe.

Enter the dungeon in front of you. As soon as you enter it, you will be confronted by something. It can be a strange being or a question or riddle that would be impossible to answer. Whatever comes up to you, simply say the magical chant: *Emeno Extrosa.* Say it repeatedly, and you will soon be transported into another plane of existence — you will be transported into Middle Earth.

Middle Earth is a legend, but it very much exists in the astral realm. It is a place of pure nature — nature greens and vast forests, as well as oceans so wide beyond what the eyes could reach. Keep your mind open and allow Middle Earth to reveal itself to you.

Once you reach Middle Earth, as usual, explore it for a while to get used to the place. The reason why so many magical practitioners do not find the Wand of Terra even after reaching Middle Earth is because the Wand of Terra is not found, but it is asked. You have to talk to the green goblin. The green goblin could be found in a small cave up the mountain located in the north of Middle Earth. As soon as you enter Middle Earth, do not change your direction, but just head straight from wherever you may find yourself. Directions in the astral realm can be tricky, so just keep in mind to keep going straight as soon as you reach this magical place.

You will soon find a mountain. Go up this mountain, and you will find a small cave. Enter the cave. Be quiet as the green goblin hates noise. You will easily find the green goblin for it is only a small cave. He will most likely be sitting in the corner either meditating or writing. As soon as you find him, say the following magical chant: *Elementari Terra Wanda.* Do not say anything else. If the green goblin asks you a question, do not answer it and wait until he gives up asking. When this happens, he will hand you the Wand of Terra. Do not say anything to the green goblin;

otherwise, the wand will disappear. Just take the wand and get out of the cave. Once you are out of the cave, you can either explore Middle Earth more or simply return to your body.

Once again, to return to your body, simply think of your physical body, and then gently bring your awareness back to your physical body. Once you can feel your body, slowly move your fingers and toes, and then very gently open your eyes and enjoy the Wand of Terra that is now in your hand.

Ifrit Wand

The Ifrit wand is another rare astral wand. It is a lot more challenging to obtain than the other wands mentioned in this book, but it is very much worth trying every now and then. This wand rightfully belongs to the fire element, and it is a very powerful wand infused with very high-quality fire energy.

The Ifrit Wand can be obtained by facing no other than the mythological character Ifrit himself, who is one of the gods of fire. Although known only by many to exist in fictional mythology, it should be noted that Ifrit is very much real. It just so happens that his dimensional existence is in the astral plane. This is not surprising for trained magical practitioners since many spiritual beings can really only be found in the astral dimension.

To meet the fire-god Ifrit, one should enter the Volcano of Hephaestus. This volcano is located in the astral realm, and the way to access it involves magical travel with your imagination. You should already know how to do this by now, but how do you reach the Volcano of Hephaestus? And how can you find Ifrit once you reach it? Here are the steps:

Assume a comfortable position and relax. Close your eyes and free the mind. Once you are feeling relaxed, imagine a staircase in front of you. See and feel that you are slowly walking and descending the steps. As you go deeper and deeper, feel yourself accessing a deeper state of mind. The only way to reach the Volcano of Hephaestus is through a deep state of mind. If you cannot reach a deep state of mind, you will not be able to travel to and reach the said magical volcano. Do not rush this process. It is important that you reach a deep state of mind. Once you feel that you are ready, stop walking down the stairs, and simply clear your mind.

Now, gently chant the name of the volcano: *Volcano of Hephaestus*. As you are doing this, use your willpower to be transported into it. If you have reached the right state of mind, then you will be instantly transported into this magical volcano. Take some time to just observe it. For now, just explore the place and get used to it.

As you look around, you may see a wooden door. This is the passageway into the volcano. Enter through this wooden door. Just follow the way, and you will soon reach a room where the giant Ifrit sits on his throne. his throne. As soon as you see him, remember never to look him in the eye. Keep your head low, but be sure to remain confident. Never forget that you are a magus.

He may test you several times. There are no rules on how he will do it. When this happens, just be open and do your best to succeed. If Ifrit is pleased, he may grant you the Ifrit wand.

You might think that this is very easy and simple. Indeed, it is simple, but it is not easy. The final test of Ifrit involves having to face him yourself, and it involves surviving his powerful fire psychic attack without putting up any defense. This means that if he attacks you, just hold your ground and take all the attacks. Indeed, the Ifrit Wand is not for complete beginners.

f you manage to pass all his tests, especially the final test, Ifrit himself will give you the Ifrit Wand. Once you have the Ifrit Wand, that is the only time when you can look him in the eye. Once you obtain the wand, thank Ifrit, and then you could easily leave and return to your body with the wand. As soon as you return, be sure to give a name to your Ifrit Wand.

The Ifrit Wand is a very powerful fire wand. Be sure to use it wisely and responsibly. It is also worth noting that the Ifrit Wand is a living astral wand.

Best Practices

Let us now discuss the essential best practices that you can observe with regard to astral magic wands:

Keep Looking

There may be days when you might not be able to find an astral wand. When this happens, do not be discouraged. Instead, just keep looking and keep trying. You will surely find one (or even more) soon. Having the conscious intention to look for a wand while you journey in the astral dimension can also help attract the right energy.

Meditate

The practice of meditation is strongly advised, especially if you are serious about having any real progress in your magical and spiritual life. It is also recommended to meditate before you search for a wand. Meditation will take and keep you in the right mindset for magical work. The practice of meditation will also naturally develop your overall psychic and magical faculties.

Build a relationship with your wand

If you are using a living wand, know that it is inhabited by a spirit, being, or entity. Indeed, it is very much alive. By establishing a closer relationship with your living wand, you can significantly increase its effectiveness. A good way to do this is simply by using your wand as often as you can, and also by talking to it. You may talk to your wand out loud or even telepathically.

A GUIDE TO ACQUIRING AN ASTRAL MAGIC WAND

Know that by doing so, you are actually communicating to the spirit, being, or entity that is inhabiting your living wand.

Learn from your wand

This is true, especially if you are using a living wand. Many people think that magical practitioners simply use their wands; but it is not always about using the wand, for we can also learn from our wand. Let your living wand teach you. The being or entity that lives there is pure magic, and you can learn from it. Keep an open mind, so that you can receive messages from the Otherworld.

A magic wand is only a tool

Although working with magic wands can be so interesting and fun, never forget that wands are still just a tool. The real magic comes from you. The best weapon of the magus is still the mind, for all true and most genuine magic starts and ends in the mind. Although wands can be helpful in magic, it is not good to rely on them completely. Never forget that you are still the magus.

Do not forget to recharge your wand

Wands require energy for them to function effectively. It is a good practice to recharge your wand every now and then. This is true even if a wand already has the ability to exist permanently. It is still good to recharge your wand to make sure that it has enough magical energy to do whatever task you may assign to it.

Take advantage of the benefits of an astral wand

Unlike a physical wand, an astral wand can be used anywhere, and you can bring it with you everywhere. In fact, there are advanced magical practitioners who actively use their astral wands in public, casting powerful magic without catching the attention of the crowd. So, make use of your astral wand whenever possible. The more that you use it, the more that you will develop your magic wand skills.

Keep a notebook

If you intend to use several wands, it is a good practice to keep a notebook or journal. This way, you can organize your wands easily and monitor them. You must keep your notebook private. For added security, you should use a code when writing the name of your wands. This way, even if someone else sees your notebook, they will not know about the name of your magic wands. Remember that names have power. Through the use of the name, magical manipulations can be made. Therefore, be sure to keep the name of your magic wands a secret.

Enjoy the journey

The magical journey is endless. Do not rush the learning process. Continue learning and making your own discoveries. This book is only a key that will open a door of magic that leads to various magical kingdoms. Enjoy every step of the journey. And, whenever you feel that you are not good enough or simply do not belong, just remember this ancient magical wisdom: You are magic.

A Call to Christ

Before we part, I would like to share with you someone who is very important to me. He saved me when all my magic could no longer do it for me, and He is Jesus Christ. I would like to invite you, my dear reader, to kindly give it a try, give Christ a chance. Who knows, He might just change your life forever.

I would suggest that you forget about everything that you think you know about Him, and just start with a clean slate. Get to know Him on your own. A good start is by reading the gospels in the Bible. I strongly suggest that you start by reading the Book of Matthew, which also happens to be the first book in the New Testament.

Even today, many witches and wizards are turning to Jesus for more magic, as well as for a more genuine spirituality. It is also worth noting that shortly after Christ was born, He was visited by the three magi, which many people today refer to as the three kings or the three wise men. However, in the original text, the word that is used is *magi*, and the word *magi* is the plural form of the word *magus* from which the word *magic* came from. As you can see, Jesus was visited by three magical practitioners.

We can also visit Christ today. We just have to be open to Him; and He, in fact, is the One who will come to us. Forget about what religions have said about Him, for you can come to Him personally, and He will manifest Himself to you. I hope you may give this a chance. Jesus is God. I know it now, and I know that He loves you, too. Blessed Be.

Don't miss out!

Visit the website below and you can sign up to receive emails whenever Merryl Kowalska publishes a new book. There's no charge and no obligation.

https://books2read.com/r/B-A-OMZV-CRHDC

BOOKS 2 READ

Connecting independent readers to independent writers.

Also by Merryl Kowalska

Immersive Magic
A Guide to Acquiring an Astral Magic Wand